Written by
Gillian Clements

Scholastic Children's Books,
Commonwealth House, 1-19 New Oxford Street,
London WC1A 1NU, UK
a division of Scholastic Ltd
London ~ New York ~ Toronto ~ Sydney ~ Auckland

First published in the UK by Scholastic Ltd, 1998

ISBN 0 590 19798 3

Printed by Cox & Wyman Ltd, Reading, Berks.

10 9 8 7 6 5 4 3 2 1

Contents:

Loads and loads and loads of letters

Calligraphy – you see that word in all the art shops. But what's it all about? It all sounds like a load of Greek. And it is! 'Callos' means beautiful in Greek, and 'graphia' means writing, so ... calligraphy is the art of beautiful writing.

If you keep your eyes peeled, you can see beautiful writing and lively lettering all around you. Next time you're out and about, try looking:

1. on GRAVESTONES.
You may not want to hang around these too long, but they are DEAD interesting!

2. on your 25-metre swimming CERTIFICATE.
Yes, maybe.

3. on those REALLY OLD YELLOW BOOKS written by monks.

4. on Queen Elizabeth I's CHEQUEBOOKS.
Hmm, yes, worth a try if she had any.

5. on old shop fronts, fairgrounds and HOLLYWOOD POSTERS.
Yes, definitely.

6. on £5 notes.
Yes, if you can keep them long enough for really CLOSE inspection. Or...

7. on NONE of the above.

No, not if you've kept your eyes peeled. Anyone who's stupid enough to go in for peeling their eyeballs won't be seeing anything for ages. Yuk!

Inventing words

OK. So when did all this writing begin, who invented it ... and why? No, it wasn't some old teacher who wanted to torture us with spelling tests. In fact, no-one really knows.

But writing is very ancient. If you'd been around 5,000 years ago and handed a lump of clay and a little stick to the nearest old Sumerian* farmer, he might have written the following:

He'd scratch picture symbols into the soft clay with the stick. (Sticks or reeds made excellent pens. I don't know if he ever tried writing with a goat. I doubt it. Too heavy.)

*Sumerian is the name for a very ancient peoples who lived in and around Mesopotamia (that's Iraq to you).

Fortunately, things have advanced a bit since Sumerian times, and we don't have to dig up the back garden every time we want to write something down. Today, cool calligraphers have some pretty useful things called pens (just see the two in this pack, for starters!) and a whole set of rules about how to use them. These rules aren't too complicated, but if you want to be a cool calligrapher too, you'd better read them!

Some basic rules about lettering

1. Think carefully about what kind of nib size you need for the job in hand. If you're designing a poster, for example, you don't want a fine nib or nobody will be able to read what you've written. You'll need a big, heavy nib for some big, heavy lettering! But don't worry, your free Brat Pack calligraphy pens should be suitable for most of the activities here.

2. Once you've chosen your nib, there are still some nifty tricks you can use to make lettering look heavier or lighter. The smaller you write with your nib, the heavier the letters will seem:

abc abc

3. You get those thick and thin lines in your letters by holding your pen and nib at the correct angle. WATCH OUT FOR THIS SIGN!

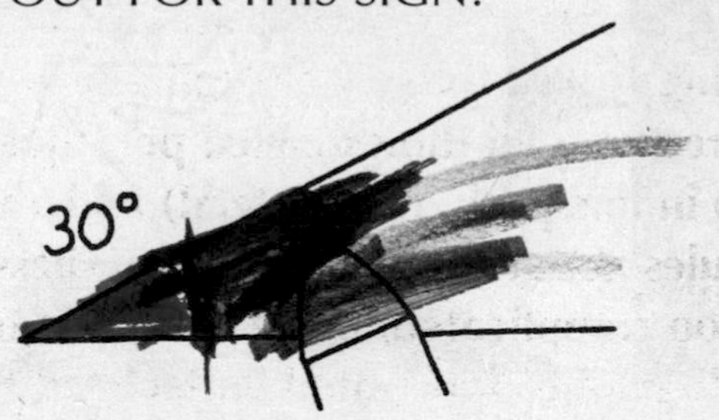

4. Be a copycat! It's really important to draw the lines and curves of your lettering as accurately as possible, so try to copy out lettering as near as possible to the original.

5. Stroke order. Some letters have to be written using more than one stroke, sometimes three or four! Watch out for the numbers and arrows.

6. Serifs. No, these are nothing to do with the Sheriff of Nottingham. These are extra lines that some letter styles have to give them a nice, arty finish.

7. Spacing between words, and between each letter is really important if you want your writing to look right. See what we mean?

Tooclosetogether

T o o f a r a p a r t

8. To make sure things stay as neat and tidy as possible, a pencil and ruler always come in handy to mark out lines to write on.

9. Paste-ups and layouts. Work out the shapes you want your finished words to make, by cutting out your practice lettering, and sticking it down like this:

10. A final note of warning for all those extra-special, creative types out there. Yes, the left-handers! Sometimes you're in danger of smudging your lettering, but if you ask, plenty of art shops will sell special calligraphy nibs especially for you. Try writing with your paper at an angle, too.

Phew! If you can remember all that, you're just about ready to get stuck into a calligraphy frenzy. Just one last thing – you might need to get your equipment ready first.

What you will need:

It's best to be prepared before you start. You know what it's like when you need something immediately and it's not there. And for those really messy and tricky jobs, borrow an adult (don't worry, you'll be able to return them afterwards). Here are some things that might come in useful:

- **Your totally unique Brat Pack felt-tip calligraphy pens! One has a fine nib and the other has a medium nib – perfect for some frenzied calligraphy practice!**
- **Dip pens. These are the posh version of calligraphy pens. You can get all sorts of different size nibs, and you dip the nib into a bottle of ink before writing. They make things a bit more interesting, but don't worry if you can't get any – you've still got your brilliant Brat Pack pens!**
- **Gold felt tip (though any colour will do)**
- **Wire (you can get this from a hardware shop)**
- **Pencil and eraser (should have these knocking around in your pencil case!)**

✎ **Paints. There are lots of different types that will come in useful for your calligraphy – poster paint, acrylic, gouache, even ceramic paints and fabric paints if you can get hold of them.**

✒ **Paintbrushes**

✎ **Paper, paper and more paper! Layout paper, graph paper, cartridge paper, brown paper ... just see what's around the house. And, of course, newspaper to cover your surfaces.**

- Cardboard
- Modelling clay
- Craft knife (ouch! be careful!)
- Scissors

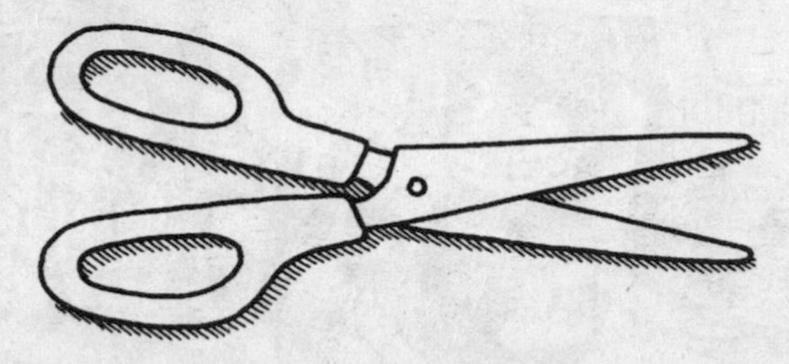

- Ruler (metal is best)
- PVA glue and gluestick

- Rubber bands
- Masking film and masking fluid
- Matt varnish
- Compasses

Well, it looks like gobbledygook to us, but some of the ancient writings that we can still see today, meant something to someone once upon a time. Difficult to believe, I know, but it's true.

Some of the earliest 'writing' was based on pictures. When people didn't have an alphabet, the easiest way to write about, say, a cow was to draw a picture of it.

How many cows? Well, make as many marks next to it as you need:

It's unlikely that *you* own any cows, but you could make a list of your things, using the Sumerian's technique.

Make your very own Sumerian-style tablet

You will need:

- **plasticine or modelling clay**
- **a thin stick or modelling tool to write with**
- **matt varnish**

What you will need to do:

1. Roll out the modelling clay to about 1cm thickness, and try to shape it to look like an ancient tablet. You could even add a few cracks and chips to make it look more authentic!

2. Decide what you're going to include in your list of belongings, and practise drawing them on some practice paper (anything you can find lying around the house). You need to keep the pictures as simple as possible, because they'll be quite difficult to score into the clay.

3. Using your stick, scratch your picture language into the clay tablet.

4. Leave the clay to set and varnish. Ask someone if they can read the list! You could do a shopping list for your grown-up, and present it to him/her next time they go shopping (if they've got the strength to carry it)!

Every picture tells a story

Stone Age people used pictures for more complicated things than lists. They managed to tell whole stories – but not ones you'd find in a book. Their stories were drawn on the walls of caves and included paintings of ferocious beasts!

Sometimes pictures of things turned into pictures of words and sounds and got called fancy names like 'Pictographs' or 'Hieroglyphs' (think of Egyptian drawings).That's still plain old picture-writing to you and me.

Rockin' Rebus!

A 'rebus' is a style of picture-writing that represents sounds. You can invent your own, but first, see if you can understand these:

1.

2.

Answers: **1.** I saw some bees at 5 o'clock. **2.** I came, I saw, I conquered.

Many rebuses would be painted onto rocks or slabs of rock. See if you can make your own 'rock' out of modelling clay and paint your very own rebus message on it!

You will need:

- **pencil and paper to work out your design**
- **modelling clay**
- **poster or gouache paints**
- **paintbrushes**
- **varnish**

What you will need to do:

1. Work out your rebus message on paper. If you're having problems, you can always call in the help of a friend or a grown-up.

2. Roll out your modelling clay and mould it into the rock shape that you think works best.

3. Leave the clay to set. Once it's dry, draw on your design in pencil.

4. Use black paint and a thin brush to draw in the outlines, then colour in and varnish.

5. Admire your new pictographs!

If you think our alphabet is a pain to learn, with just 26 characters (you might know them as letters), then thank your lucky stars you weren't born in China. The poor old Chinese have to mug up on 50,000 characters in their alphabet!

The first known alphabet was invented 3,000 years ago by another ancient peoples called the Phoenicians. The Greeks copied them and the Romans copied them to invent their own alphabets. The Romans did a pretty good job of taking over the world, so their alphabet became known by a lot of people. After all, the Romans had loads of big hairy soldiers to make sure that people learnt their alphabet!

When they weren't frightening people, the Romans invented square capitals that were easy to chisel into bits of stone all over their Empire. Straight lines were easier to chisel than curves.

Make your own Roman capital

You will need:

- graph paper or layout paper
- fine Brat Pack calligraphy pen
- modelling clay
- rolling pin
- craft knife
- varnish

What you will need to do:

1. Look at the Roman square capitals at the back of this book, and choose which letter you want to draw. It could be your initial. Practise drawing it on graph paper, or layout paper that you've drawn guidelines on, using your Brat Pack calligraphy pen.

2. Hold your pen at the angles shown at the back of the book. Most letters will take more than one stroke, but if you follow the order of the stroke numbers at the back of the book you shouldn't have too many problems. And watch out for serifs – you'll need to add them at the end!

3. Practise drawing your letter lots of times until you think you've got it right. Then carefully cut out your best attempt.

4. Roll out your modelling clay to about 2-3cm thick and lay your letter on top. Trace round it, keeping the letter shape nice and accurate.

5. Carefully cut your letter out of the clay, using the craft knife. Make sure an adult is close at hand. Don't forget the serifs – you don't want to chop them off!

6. Leave your clay letter to dry, then varnish. If you can attach a loop of wire to the back, this would make a great sign for your bedroom door!

A brush with graffiti

Roman stone inscriptions were all very well, but your average Roman citizen couldn't carry a slab of rock and a chisel around with him, ready to carve a quick note to his chum. And budding graffiti artists weren't going to wait 1900 years for spray cans to be invented. Instead, people began to write with brushes and reed pens. And they'd use any surface that came to hand – papyrus paper, wax tablets ... and walls! Because of this new way of writing, new 'Rustic' letters became fashionable. Rustic letters were taller, thinner and faster letters to write than square capitals. Just the job for a vandal in a hurry!

Do you want to be a Roman vandal, too? Yes? Then...

Make your own graffiti on a mug!

You will need:

- **a plain mug (one your grown-up doesn't mind you using)**
- **stiff-bristled brush**
- **tracing paper**
- **medium Brat Pack calligraphy pen**
- **black pen, biro, pencils**
- **sticky-backed plastic**
- **masking tape**
- **ceramic paint**

What you will need to do:

1. Decide what you're going to write on your mug (nothing too long!) and practise writing it with the rustic letters.

2. Cut out some tracing paper so that it will fit snugly around the mug.

3. Trace the outline of your message onto tracing paper using a black pen. Then scribble over the outline in pencil. Transfer your message onto the sticky-back masking film by taping your message backwards onto the masking film's paper backing. Go over the outlines very hard with a pencil or biro and the letter marks will show up.

4. Cut out the message from the masking film very carefully. Try not to tear the plastic!

5. Peel off the film packing and stick your stencil onto the mug. Some tape will keep it secure.

6. Read the ceramic paint instructions*, then apply to the mug through the stencil. Leave the paint to dry.

7. You could cut out lots of other stencils to illustrate your message – stars, moons, crosses or flower shapes all work well!

*The ceramic paint that needs heating looks best.

In the 13th-15th centuries (ie zillions of years ago) lots of monks sat at high desks copying out 'illuminated manuscripts'. No, these weren't books that came with a free torch – they were highly-decorated books all painstakingly written out by hand.

But the monks weren't the only ones who suffered for their art. Birds and animals had to make their contribution too:

- Hides from cows, goats and even squirrels were used to make parchment...
- swans and geese were plucked of their feathers to make quill pens...

- and blood was used as ink!

Did you know?

1. That the writing end of the feather was shaped into a nib with a little knife, and that's how penknives got their name.

2. That a busy medieval scribe had to re-cut his quill 60-70 times a day!

Make your own patterned cards and paper

What you will need:

- **your own dip pen or Brat Pack calligraphy pen**
- **ink or paints if necessary**
- **paper to practise on**
- **white or coloured thin card**
- **brown or plain wrapping paper**
- **pencil**

What you will need to do:

1. Practise! Monks had to do this for years before they got it right. Hold your pen at the correct angle and have a go at the thick and thin lines. Remember to keep your hand relaxed, or you might have one too many squiggles! You can make these patterns without lifting your pen off the paper – they're one-stroke patterns.

2. Or you can try these patterns. These need more than one pen stroke, so follow the arrows!

3. Once you've found a pattern you like, decide what you want to decorate first. You can make writing paper, wrapping paper, greeting cards, bookmarks ... there's loads of things for a budding calligrapher to create!

If you're after a more authentic look (brilliant for fooling people with treasure maps and old wills), then you'll need some parchment paper. You won't want to start skinning the nearest cat, but there is an easier way of creating that ancient look...

Fake your own olde parchment

What you will need:

- cartridge paper
- cold, used tea bags
- stiff cardboard
- parcel tape

What you will need to do:

1. Damp the back of your cartridge paper all over with a clean, moist sponge or dishcloth.

2. Find some stiff card to use as a work surface and lay your cartridge paper down on top of it. Tape the corners of your paper down to the card with some parcel tape to stop the corners from curling up.

3. Pick up your damp, soggy tea bags and make interesting tea stains/olde-type marks to look like parchment.

4. Leave the stained paper to dry, then peel it away from the cardboard, ready to start creating your authentic document!

Did you know?

1. Real gold leaf was often used in illuminated manuscripts. It never fades and is beaten so thin that you can eat it – it just dissolves on the tongue!

2. Scribes used lions' teeth to buff up gold leaf, though cats' and dogs' teeth would do.

3. Dragons' blood made very good red paint (so they say).

Fake your own illuminated manuscript

What you will need:

- parchment paper (you've just made some, remember?)
- fine Brat Pack calligraphy pen
- gold felt-tip
- coloured paints or ink
- paintbrush
- pencil and ruler

What you will need to do:

1. Sketch out your design for the illuminated manuscript. Animals, flowers and different patterns were often used to illustrate these books.

2. The first letter of your writing needs to go really big. We're talking giant-sized!

Carefully draw it out in pencil, then go over the

outline with black pen. Fill the inside in with your gold felt-tip – or any other colour you like.

3. Now fill in the rest of your page with whatever you want to write. But remember, your calligraphy needs to be as neat and tidy as possible, so concentrate!

4. The best for last! Add your pictures and patterns to decorate the borders of the page. But don't go mad – you still want to read what you've written!

OK, you've had enough practice by now. Here's your chance to prove just how creative you can get, with these amazing calligraphy ideas:

Music maestro!

If you've ever lost a music tape that you've really loved (don't lie, we've all done it), then this is the activity for you!

You will need:

- **a sheet of self-adhesive labels to fit on your cassette cases**
- **acrylic or gouache paint**
- **ink**
- **pencil**
- **ruler**
- **fine Brat Pack calligraphy pen**
- **scissors**

What you will need to do:

1. Make sure that your label fits on the front of your cassette case. If it doesn't, trim it to the right size.

2. Draw a groovy picture frame all around the edge of the label and decorate. Musical notes would look good.

3. Choose what calligraphy alphabet you're going to use, and practise writing out the label on rough paper first. Then carefully fill in your cassette label – you might find it helpful to pencil in guidelines first.

4. Peel off the label and put it on your cassette case. Now stand back and admire!

Gothic horror

It was a moonless night, but out of the shadows cast by the dying light of a candle, crept the vengeful figure of ... Dracula! We've all seen those old gothic horror films – but could you design a film poster with some scary calligraphy?

Think of a good title, something like 'I was the dog of Frankenstein' (written in Gothic script), then design the poster's picture to go with it.

You will need:

- **medium Brat Pack calligraphy pen**
- **layout paper**
- **cartridge paper**
- **felt-tips for drawing**
- **pencil, ruler**
- **poster or gouache paints**

What you will need to do:

1. Think of a design for your film poster. Looking at other film posters at the cinema might help.

2. Draw your design out in rough on layout paper and practise your Gothic script with your Brat Pack calligraphy pen on ruled paper.

3. When you're happy with your script, copy it out onto your best cartridge paper. Then draw in your pictures and decoration, using poster or gouache paints to add colour. You should be able to make your poster really scary!

Hang it up and enjoy watching people jump out of their skins next time they walk into your bedroom! Of course, no film promotion is complete without a designer T-shirt to go with it! If you want to make your very own gothic horror T-shirt, then here's how to!

<u>You will need:</u>

- **old, pale-coloured plain T-shirt**
- **fabric paint**
- **card or newspaper**
- **sticky backed plastic**
- **craft knife**
- **grown-up**

<u>What you will need to do:</u>

1. Copy out your gothic film title onto the back of the sticky-backed plastic and, carefully using the craft knife, cut out your lettering. Make sure you don't cut out any inside bits of letters that are meant to be there!

2. Lay the T-shirt out flat and slide the card or newspaper inside it. This will stop the fabric paint from leaking through and staining the back of your T-shirt when you're painting it.

3. Peel away the back of the sticky-backed plastic stencil and carefully apply it to the front of your T-shirt.

4. Read the instructions for your fabric paint, and using a stiff-brushed paintbrush, apply the paint through the stencil.

5. Leave the paint to dry, and peel away your stencil from the T-shirt. You now have your very own gothic horror T-shirt!

Some day your prints will come

The Chinese invented printing in about 600, but the rest of us didn't catch up with this idea until about 1440, when a clever man called Gutenberg thought he'd move things along and invented the printing press!

If you think you'd like to follow in Gutenberg's footsteps, there are lots of fun ways to do your own printing.

<u>You will need:</u>

- **a printing block. Easier than it sounds – look in the kitchen for a spare potato, or 'borrow' a sponge from the bathroom.**

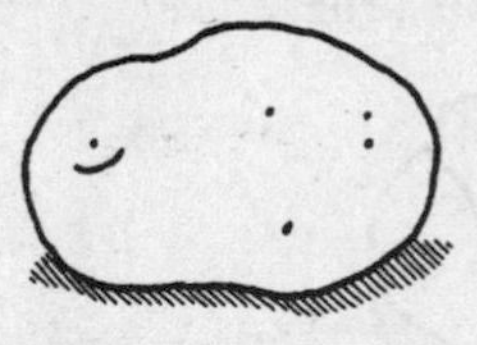

- **craft knife**
- **layout paper**
- **medium Brat Pack calligraphy pen**
- **white or coloured art or cartridge paper**
- **coloured inks or paints**
- **masking tape**
- **PVA glue and card**

What you will need to do:

1. Choose your favourite letter and style for your print, and practise drawing it. It can be nice and big, so use your medium pen.

2. When you're happy with it, cut out your best letter and, turning it round so that it's back to front, lay the letter onto your 'printing block'. This could be a potato cut in half or a bathroom sponge.

3. Keeping your adult close by, use the craft knife to cut away the sides of the potato or sponge from the edge of your back to front letter.

If you're using a sponge, it will probably need some stiff card stuck to the back of it with the PVA glue.

4. Dip your printing block into your coloured ink or paint and press onto some layout paper as a practice run, or until you've got rid of any excess paint or ink from the surface. Then decorate all kinds of different paper:

Did you know?

Leonardo da Vinci, all-round Renaissance genius and painter of the Mona Lisa, was so tremendously clever that he wrote back to front and right to left. He called it mirror-writing.

You could try your own mirror-writing. Write your name back to front and right to left (concentrate now!), then turn it over and hold it up to the light. Can you read it?

Queen Elizabeth goes loopy!

Elizabeth I of England, a bit of a Renaissance woman herself, wrote in a sort of italic, with loops and squiggles and flourishes. Try and copy her signature:

As well as curly-wurly writing, it was fashionable in Liz's day to have your portrait painted – in miniature! Then you could give your piccy to your boyfriend or girlfriend, and they could keep it close to their heart (swoon!). A bit like sending your photo to someone today.

See if you can draw your own miniature painting and add an Elizabethan signature at the bottom. Then choose a loved one to send it to!

You will need:

- **art paper**
- **layout paper**
- **coloured paints**
- **pencil, ruler**
- **black felt-tip**
- **compasses**
- **fine Brat Pack calligraphy pen**

What you will need to do:

1. With a pencil and ruler, draw out a 10cm square on your best paper.

2. Find the centre of the square by drawing a diagonal line from one corner of the square to the other. Repeat the line, running between the other two corners to make an X. The centre of your square is where the diagonal lines cross. This should mark the middle of your portrait area. Then cut the square out.

3. Using your compasses, make two circles on the paper, one inside the other. The outer circle should be 5cm across, and the one inside 3cm across. This gives you a frame for your portrait.

4. Colour in the frame a suitable colour – yellow or gold would be good. Then draw in your own self-portrait. Remember, you don't have a lot of room so you might not be able to draw in every single hair on your head!

5. Now for your loopy signature! Look at Queen Elizabeth I's and at the loopy italic alphabet. Practise your own on layout paper, then when it's just right, copy it out below your portrait.

6. Give your portrait to your chosen loved one and send their heart a-flutter!

What the Dickens?

What the Dickens is this? Well, it's Copperplate Script, and the point is lots of engravers liked it because they used a fine point for all its loops and squiggles. It really flourished on graves too:

Generations of Victorian schoolchildren and clerks like Bob Cratchit in Charles Dickens' *Christmas Carol,* were brought up on a diet of Copperplate ... so what better style for this snazzy restaurant menu? Of course, you don't have to own a restaurant to use these menus. Try writing your own version to go on the dining room table next time mum or dad serve up dinner! They'll think you're dead posh!

Bob Cratchit's Victorian Eatorium Menu

Christmas Carol Fayre

4 calling birds

3 French hens

2 turtle doves

and a partridge in a pear sauce

All served with a holly and ivy garnish

Tiny Tim's Children's Fayre

Tiny portions of the above

Scrooge's Economy Fayre

Gruel

Crust of stale bread

Glass of water (optional)

What you will need:
for the menu

- **pencil, ruler**
- **layout paper**
- **art paper**
- **fine Brat Pack calligraphy pen**
- **masking tape or sellotape**

for the cover

- **thin, coloured card**
- **coloured paper**
- **a piece of stiff card**
- **string**
- **PVA glue**
- **thin paintbrush**
- **coloured wax crayon**
- **scissors**

What you will need to do:

1. Think up a name for your restaurant and the menu you're going to have. They can be funny or serious.

2. Look at your Copperplate script alphabet and practise writing it, following the guidelines very carefully.

Blackbird Pie
Curds and Wh

3. Cut out a piece of layout paper 24cm x 16cm and draw lines across where you want to write out your dishes. Draw a line down the middle of the paper, and this will help you to make sure you get everything dead in the centre of the page. Using a fine nib, practise writing out your menu.

4. Once you're happy that everything looks just as you want it, write out the menu again. But this time, do it on your art paper.

For the menu cover:

1. With a thin paintbrush, write out your restaurant initials in glue onto thick card. They have to fill your cover (which will be 25cm x 17cm) so make them nice and big!

2. Press string into your glue letters, cutting it where necessary, and leave to dry.

3. Next, place a piece of coloured paper over the string and make a nice 'wax rubbing' of your initials by rubbing over the paper with your wax crayon. Try not to press down too hard, or you'll crease the paper.

4. Cut out your menu cover from the thin card. It should be 34cm x 25cm, then fold in half. Stick your restaurant initials onto the front of the cover and pop your menu inside. Congratulations! You are now the proud owner of a totally unique and tempting menu. All you need now is someone to cook the food!

It's catching!

You might find that after impressing your friends with all your calligraphy creations, calligraphy is catching! There might be lots of people who suddenly want to start borrowing your calligraphy pens and stealing your ideas. But there's no need to get your knickers in a twist, because the one really incredible thing about calligraphy, is that it is totally unique.

Every piece of calligraphy you do is a completely original one off! No two pieces will ever be exactly the same. If you aren't convinced, try writing your name out twice. Now take a close look. There are bound to be some differences, no matter how small they are. And if you keep it up and become really good, who knows where your calligraphy will end up...

- ✎ **appearing on *The Antiques Roadshow***
- ✒ **hanging in a museum**
- ✎ **wrapping up the fish and chips**

So, as long as you can keep thinking up new ideas for things to do, your calligraphy frenzy will keep you going for ages!

Sensational scripts

On the next few pages, you'll find four different scripts (styles of writing) that have been used in the activities – Roman, Rustic, Gothic and Copperplate. You can use these to help you write your own calligraphy – either by tracing over them or copying them out. The pen angle signs show you which way to hold your pen and the numbered arrows show you what pen strokes to make and in which order. Now, get scribbling!

Roman.

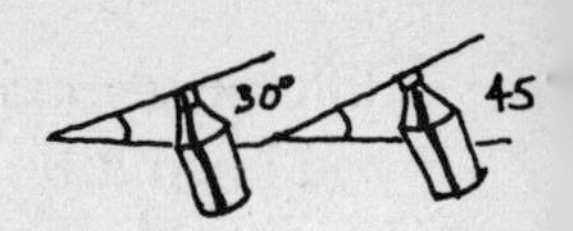

ABCDE

FGHIJK

LMNOP

QRSTU

VWXYZ

B A O M
A B C D E
F G H I J K
L M N O P
Q R S T U
V W X Y Z

Rustic.

A B C D E F

60°

G H I J K L

80°

M N O P Q

45°

R S T U V

W X Y Z

Gothic.

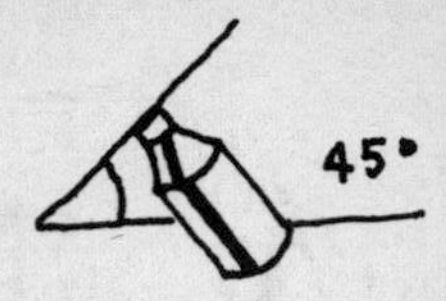

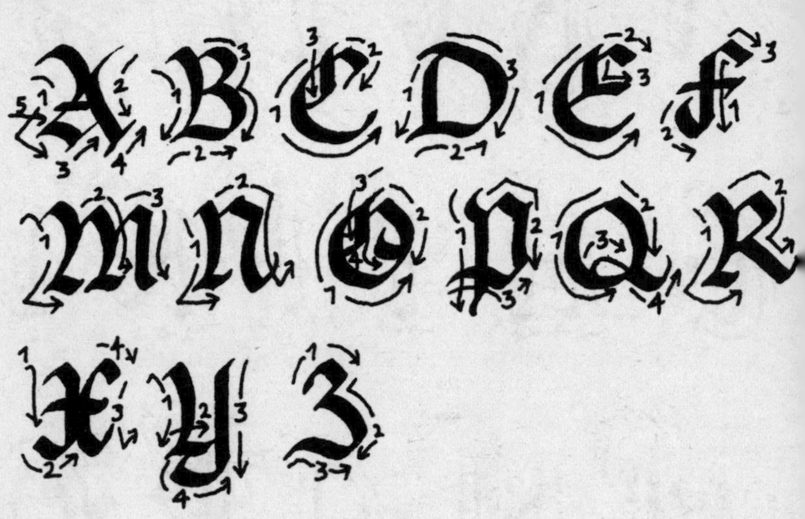

a b c d e f g h i

j k l m n o p q r

s t u v w x y z

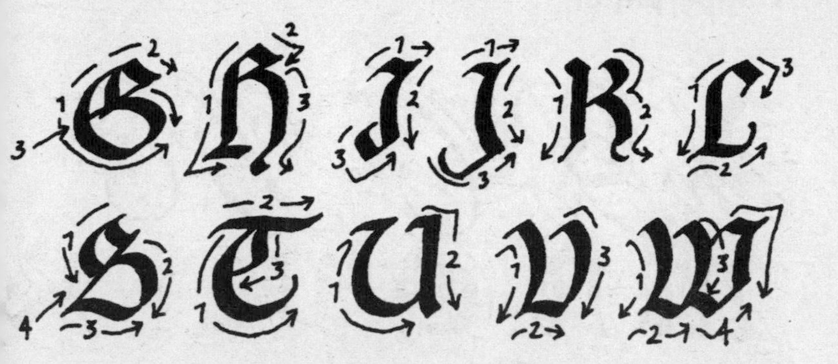

A couple of more fancy bits you can use:

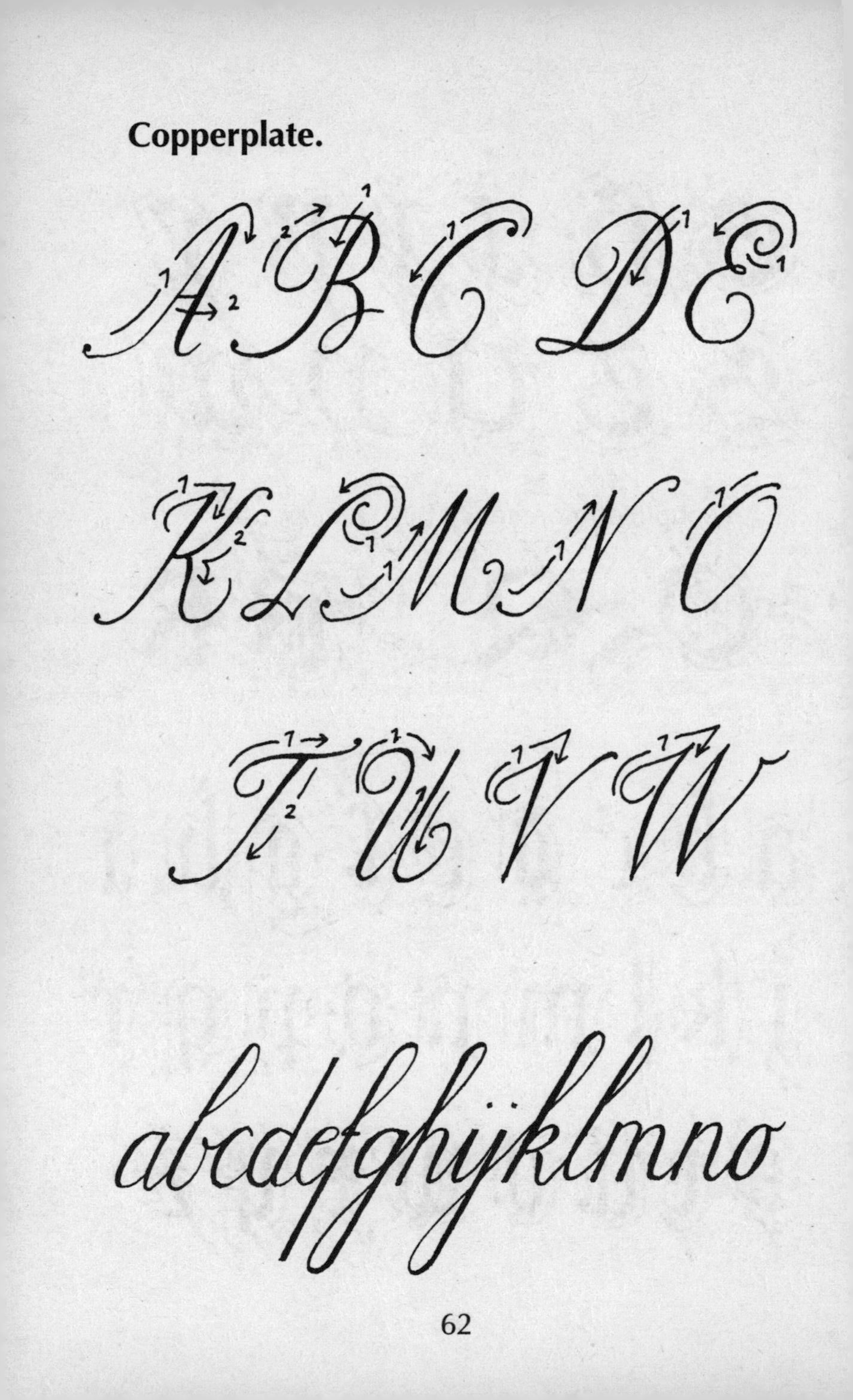

Copperplate.

A B C D E

K L M N O

T U V W

abcdefghijklmno

F G H I J

P Q R S

X Y Z

pqrstuvwxyz

Get your hands on some more Brat Packs,
and keep yourself busy:

Do you want to look a bug in the eye?
You can with the free bug box!

Stamp Mania!

With a self-inking star stamp, you can
make loads of cool pressies.

Grow giant flowers, flowers you can eat ...
and square tomatoes!

Make your own completely unique
beads and bangles.

PRACTICAL JOKES

With a free false spider and squirty thing
you'll never stop laughing!